# Kentucky

by Xavier W. Niz

**Consultant:**
Micheal A. Hudson
Collections Branch Manager
Kentucky Historical Society

Capstone
press
Mankato, Minnesota

Capstone Press
151 Good Counsel Drive • P.O. Box 669 • Mankato, Minnesota 56002
http://www.capstone-press.com

*Library of Congress Cataloging-in-Publication Data*
Niz, Xavier W.
    Kentucky / Xavier W. Niz.
    v. cm.—(Land of liberty)
    Includes bibliographical references and index.
    Contents: About Kentucky—The land, climate, and wildlife—History
of Kentucky—Government and politics—Economy and resources—People
and culture.
    ISBN 0-7368-1585-6 (hardcover)
    1. Kentucky—Juvenile literature. [1. Kentucky.] I. Title. II. Series.
F451.3 .N59 2003
976.9—dc21                                        2002013992

Summary: An introduction to the geography, history, government, politics, economy,
resources, people, and culture of Kentucky, including maps, charts, and a recipe.

**Editorial Credits**
Blake A. Hoena, editor; Jennifer Schonborn, series designer; Linda Clavel, book
    designer; Angi Gahler, illustrator; Deirdre Barton, photo researcher; Eric
    Kudalis, product planning editor

**Photo Credits**
Cover images:horse farm near Lexington, Kent & Donna Dannen; Louisville
skyline, Index Stock Imagery/David Davis

Capstone Press/Gary Sundermeyer, 54; Corbis/Bettmann, 29, 36, 45, 50;
Corbis/Brownie Harris, 42; Corbis/Charles E. Rotkin, 30; Corbis/David Muench,
16; Corbis/Kit Houghton, 56; Corbis/Lowell Georgia, 44; Corbis/Raymond
Gehman, 8; Corbis/Reuters NewMedia Inc., 4; Getty Images Sport Services/Jed
Jacobsohn, 51; Hulton Archive by Getty Images/Marion Post Wolcott, 18,
26–27; Index Stock Imagery/David Davis, 46; Index Stock Imagery/Charlie
Borland, 48; Index Stock Imagery/Jeff Greenberg, 15; Kent & Donna Dannen,
12–13, 40–41, 52–53, 63; Library of Congress, 24; One Mile Up, Inc., 55 (both);
PhotoDisc, Inc./Alan and Sandy Carey, 14; Robert McCaw, 57; Stock Montage,
Inc., 23, 37, 58; UNICORN Stock Photos/Andre Jenny, 20, 38; UNICORN
Stock Photos/Chris Boylan, 32; U.S. Postal Service, 59

**Design Elements**
Corbis, Digital Stock, Digital Vision, PhotoDisc, Inc.

1 2 3 4 5 6 08 07 06 05 04 03

# Table of Contents

The horse War Emblem won the 2002 Kentucky Derby.

# Chapter 1

# About Kentucky

On the first Saturday in May, more than 100,000 people gather in Louisville to watch the Kentucky Derby. This race is the oldest continually run horse race in the United States. Race day is known as "Derby Day."

The Kentucky Derby Festival begins two weeks before Derby Day. The festival starts with the Thunder Over Louisville air show. Pilots and skydivers perform for the show's audience. At night, a large fireworks show takes place.

Many other events are held during the festival. A hot-air balloon race begins at the Kentucky Fair and Exposition Center. Steamships race up and down the Ohio River. The Pegasus Parade is held in downtown Louisville.

On Derby Day, people gather at Churchill Downs racetrack. They come to watch some of the world's fastest racehorses compete. The race covers 1.25 miles (2 kilometers) and lasts around two minutes. Race fans say it is "the greatest two minutes in sports."

## The Bluegrass State

Kentucky's nickname is the "Bluegrass State." It earned this name from a type of grass that grows in northern Kentucky. Bluegrass is actually dark green, but it produces blue-colored flowers in spring. When seen from a distance, the flowers make the grass look blue.

Seven states border Kentucky. Indiana and Ohio are to the north. West Virginia and Virginia share Kentucky's eastern border. Tennessee lies to the south. Missouri and Illinois are west of Kentucky. Kentucky is the 37th largest state in the country.

Today, more than 4 million people live in Kentucky. Some Kentuckians can trace their ancestry back to America's first European settlers. Others are descendants of African American slaves or American Indians.

# Kentucky Cities

Kentucky has a colorful history. It is filled with stories of pioneers like Thomas Walker and Daniel Boone. Revolutionary War (1775–1783) and Civil War (1861–1865) battles were fought in Kentucky. The state also has suffered conflicts over tobacco farming, coal mining, and civil rights.

The Cumberland Mountains are part of the Appalachian Plateau in eastern Kentucky.

# Chapter 2

# Land, Climate, and Wildlife

Kentucky is in the east-central United States. The state is divided into five land regions. These areas are the Appalachian Plateau, the Bluegrass Region, the Mississippi Plateau, the Western Coal Field, and the Jackson Purchase.

## The Land

Eastern Kentucky is part of the Appalachian Plateau. This mountainous area has many high ridges and narrow valleys. Forests cover much of the region. The Cumberland and Pine Mountains are within the Appalachian Plateau. Black Mountain is part of the Cumberland Mountains. It rises 4,139 feet

(1,262 meters) above sea level and is the highest point in Kentucky.

In north-central Kentucky, the Bluegrass Region has many rolling hills. More than half of Kentucky's population lives there. Sandy, conelike formations called knobs lie along the southern edge of the region.

The Mississippi Plateau takes up much of south-central and southwestern Kentucky. It is the largest region in the state. This area also is called the Pennyroyal after a mint plant that grows there. Kentucky's richest farmland is found in this area. Many caves lie beneath the Mississippi Plateau.

The Western Coal Field in northwestern Kentucky is a hilly area. The eastern part of the region has many wooded ridges and rocky cliffs. The Western Coal Field is known for its large coal deposits.

The Jackson Purchase is the southwestern tip of Kentucky. People named this area after General Andrew Jackson. He bought the land from the Chickasaw Indians in 1818. Rich farmland covers most of the Jackson Purchase. Kentucky's lowest point is in this region along the Mississippi River's bank. The land is only 257 feet (78 meters) above sea level.

# Kentucky's Land Features

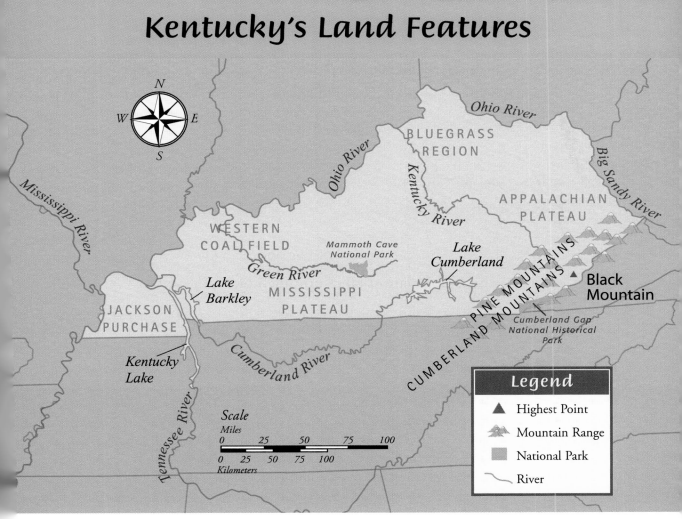

## Rivers and Lakes

Kentucky has more than 13,000 miles (20,900 kilometers) of rivers and streams. It is the only state bordered by rivers in three directions. The Big Sandy and Tug Fork Rivers flow along its eastern border. The Ohio River curves along Kentucky's northern border. The Mississippi River forms its far western border. The Cumberland River and the Tennessee River are other important rivers in Kentucky.

Rivers have played an important part in Kentucky's history. Many settlers entered the state on the Kentucky River. Early Kentuckians used rivers to ship goods to market. Many of the state's large cities were founded near rivers.

All of Kentucky's large lakes are formed by dammed rivers. Kentucky Lake and Lake Cumberland are two of the world's largest man-made lakes. Other large lakes in Kentucky include Lake Barkley and Buckhorn Lake.

## Climate

Kentuckians enjoy mild weather throughout the year. Summers are generally warm. Winters are cool but not very cold. Kentucky receives an average of 47 inches (119 centimeters) of rain and snow each year. Most precipitation falls as rain in the southern areas of the state. The mountains of southeastern Kentucky receive some snow.

## Plant Life

Forests cover almost half of Kentucky. American beech, white basswood, sweet buckeye, and Kentucky coffee trees grow in

The Kentucky River flows through eastern Kentucky. During pioneer days, settlers entered Kentucky by boat on this river.

the Appalachian Plateau. Oak, pine, gum, and hickory trees grow in the rest of the state.

Wildflowers grow throughout much of Kentucky. In spring, bluebells, violets, lady's slippers, and other wildflowers color the state. In fall, Kentucky is covered with tickseed, aster, ironweed, and goldenrod flowers.

## Wildlife

Many types of wildlife live in Kentucky. White-tailed deer are found throughout the state. A few black bears and bobcats

White-tailed deer live throughout Kentucky.

# Mammoth Cave

Mammoth Cave is the largest known cave system in the world. It stretches for 350 miles (560 kilometers) underground.

In 1941, the U.S. government created Mammoth Cave National Park. Today, more than 2 million people visit the park each year. They take tours to see Mammoth Dome and Frozen Niagara within the cave. Visitors can see strange animals like eyeless fish, white spiders, and blind beetles that live in the cave.

live in Kentucky's mountainous areas. Smaller animals such as raccoons, foxes, opossums, and rabbits are common in Kentucky's forests.

Many birds and fish can be found in Kentucky. Blue jays, crows, and Carolina chickadees are common. Great blue herons live along the Kentucky River. Catfish, bluegill, trout, and walleye all swim in Kentucky's rivers and lakes. The Kentucky bass is the state fish.

Today, people can walk along paths used by early settlers. This path through the Appalachian Mountains is called the Wilderness Road.

# Chapter 3

# History of Kentucky

In the mid-1600s, British explorers began to travel westward from the colony of Virginia. In 1654, Abraham Wood made the first recorded trip to Kentucky. At the time, several American Indian tribes lived and hunted in the area. These groups included Cherokee, Creek, Chickasaw, Shawnee, and Mingo Indians.

In 1750, explorer Thomas Walker led a group called the Loyal Land Company of Virginia into Kentucky. Walker found an old American Indian path through the Appalachian Mountains. American Indians called this trail the Warrior's Path. Walker renamed it the Cumberland Gap after the English Duke of Cumberland. The path let Walker's group easily cross the mountains. The Cumberland Gap became the gateway into the western wilderness for many settlers.

In 1774, James Harrod founded Harrodstown, Kentucky's first permanent white settlement. Pioneer Daniel Boone soon followed him. He helped found Boonesborough in 1775.

Daniel Boone was an early pioneer. He led many settlers into Kentucky along the Wilderness Road.

Boone led many groups of settlers across the Cumberland Gap and into Kentucky. The trail he led settlers along became known as the Wilderness Road.

American Indians in the area did not like white settlers taking their land. They had lived and hunted in the area for thousands of years. American Indians and settlers often fought over the land.

## Revolutionary War

In April of 1775, American colonists went to war with Great Britain. The colonists fought to gain their independence from British rule in the Revolutionary War.

During the war, many American Indians helped the British. Indians believed the white settlers would leave their lands if defeated by the British. One of the largest battles between settlers and American Indians occurred in 1778. Shawnee Indians attacked Boonesborough. The settlers were greatly outnumbered, but Daniel Boone led a successful defense of the town.

## Statehood

After the colonists won their freedom, thousands of settlers moved west to Kentucky. They founded Louisville, Lexington, and Frankfort. By 1790, Kentucky's population had grown to more than 73,000 people.

On June 1, 1792, Kentucky became the 15th state. Kentucky was the first state west of the Appalachian Mountains. Isaac Shelby was elected the state's first governor. Frankfort eventually became the state capital.

The new state grew fast. By 1840, Kentucky's population had grown to more than 750,000. Many new settlers came

Abraham Lincoln was president of the United States during the Civil War. He was born in this cabin near Hodgenville, Kentucky, in 1816.

from Europe, including German and Irish immigrants. These people were trying to escape poverty and war in their homelands. The population also grew because large numbers of African American slaves were brought to Kentucky during this time.

Kentucky's economy grew fast. Kentucky became the leading hemp-growing state. Hemp is a plant used to make products like ropes and clothes. Kentucky also was a major producer of horses, tobacco, corn, and whiskey.

## Civil War

In the mid-1800s, the issue of states' rights divided the country. Northerners thought a strong central government should make laws for the nation. Southerners thought each state should have the right to make its own laws.

Slavery was at the center of this disagreement. In the North, slavery was illegal. Southern states used slaves to work on their farms. They worried a strong central government would make slavery illegal.

Abraham Lincoln won the 1860 presidential election. He was against slavery. Southerners were afraid Lincoln would try to end slavery in the United States. Eleven Southern states decided to leave the Union. They formed the Confederate States of America, or the Confederacy. Kentucky native Jefferson Davis became the Confederacy's president. In April 1861, the United States and the Confederacy went to war.

Whites in Kentucky were divided. Kentuckians did not want to separate from the Union. Yet, they also did not want to outlaw slavery. More than 200,000 African American slaves lived in Kentucky at the time. Kentuckians fought for both the Union and the Confederacy. Kentucky also had a star in both the U.S. and the Confederate flags.

Several Civil War battles were fought in Kentucky. In January 1862, the Union defeated Confederate forces at the Battle of Mill Springs. Later that year, the Battle of Perryville was fought. It was one of the war's bloodiest battles. About 7,500 Union and Confederate soldiers were wounded or killed.

The Battle of Perryville was one of the bloodiest battles of the Civil War. It ended in a Union victory.

## Unrest in Kentucky

After the Union won the Civil War, it took Kentucky's economy awhile to recover from the war's destruction. Many of its businesses suffered.

In the late 1800s, tobacco companies lowered the prices they paid farmers for their tobacco crops. Farmers then had a difficult time making a living by selling their crops. In the

At tobacco auctions, buyers gathered in large warehouses to bid on farmers' tobacco crops.

early 1900s, some tobacco farmers joined together to fight the tobacco companies. Their struggle was called the Black Patch War. Black Patch is a tobacco-growing region of western Kentucky. Farmers in this area burned tobacco company warehouses and attacked farmers who supported the tobacco companies. The farmers' actions led to tobacco auctions. At these sales, farmers sold their crops to the highest bidder. Farmers then could earn enough money to make a living.

# Women in Kentucky

Many women have played important roles in Kentucky's history. In the late 1800s and early 1900s, Laura Clay led the Kentucky Equal Rights Association. She worked for women's rights to receive an education and to own property.

Madeline McDowell Breckinridge played an important role in the suffrage movement, which won women the right to vote. She also fought against child labor and to improve education.

Several famous women writers came from Kentucky. In 1954, Harriette Arnow published *The Dollmaker.* This book was about eastern Kentucky women who moved to the Midwest and Northeast to find work. Other Kentucky writers include Eliza Calvert Hill and Janice Holt Giles.

Women also serve important roles in state government. Georgia Powers became the first African American woman elected to Kentucky's legislature. She served from 1968 to 1988. In 1983, Martha Layne Collins became the first female governor of Kentucky.

In the early 1900s, coal mines opened in eastern and western Kentucky. Many people sold their farms to work in the mines. Mining was a dangerous job and did not pay well. Coal dust made miners sick. Accidents killed many miners.

Poor working conditions led miners to join together to form groups called unions. Union leaders fought for better working conditions and higher pay for miners. But the mining companies did not support the unions' ideas. People from the unions and the mining companies often fought about these issues. Harlan County in Kentucky became known as "Bloody

Harlan County." Some of the worst fighting between unions and mining companies occurred there. Several people were killed.

In 1938, the mining companies finally agreed to many of the unions' demands. Miners received better pay and safer working conditions.

In the early 1930s, the U.S. economy was suffering from the Great Depression (1929–1939). Many Kentuckians lost their jobs and land. In 1933, the U.S. government created the Tennessee Valley Authority (TVA). This organization created new jobs. Many Kentuckians worked for the TVA. They built

During the early 1900s, miners often lived in mining towns near the mines they worked in. Houses were run-down and living conditions were poor in some of these towns.

dams on the Tennessee and Cumberland Rivers. They also built roads throughout the area. Some Kentuckians worked in hydroelectric plants built by the TVA. Hydroelectric plants use running water to make electricity.

Slowly, Kentucky's economy improved. In 1936, the U.S. government started storing gold at Fort Knox. Jobs in food and entertainment industries were created as soldiers moved to the area to guard the gold. In 1941, the United States entered World War II (1939–1945). Kentucky's farmers grew crops to feed U.S. soldiers. The demand for coal and oil led to an increase in jobs in Kentucky's mining industries. Many people also worked making rubber, jeeps, and airplane parts for the military.

## Civil Rights

During the 1950s, African Americans began to fight for more equal rights in the United States. At the time, African Americans were treated unfairly. They could not shop at the same stores or work the same jobs as whites. African American

Police officers kept the peace while schools in Kentucky were integrated. This African American student is being sent by bus to a school with white children.

children could not attend the same schools as white children. These practices were called segregation.

In 1954, the U.S. Supreme Court ruled that segregation in public schools was illegal. People in southern states, including Kentucky, fought this ruling. But Kentucky lawmakers eventually agreed to integrate its schools. This decision forced schools to allow white and African American students to attend classes together.

Kentucky lawmakers passed the Kentucky Civil Rights Act in 1966. This law requires that all people receive equal chances for employment and housing. Kentucky was the first southern state to pass a civil rights law.

## Recent Challenges

In the 1970s, fuel shortages increased the value of Kentucky's coal industry. But coal mining can harm the environment. A type of mining called strip mining involves stripping off layers

Strip mining is a process that involves stripping away the top layers of earth.

of earth to expose the coal deposits below. Rain can wash away the loosened soil, causing erosion and water pollution. In 1978, Congress passed a law requiring mine owners to repair the land they mine.

Education has been a recent concern for Kentuckians. In June 1989, the Kentucky Supreme Court ruled that Kentucky children were not receiving a proper education. Many Kentucky students were scoring below the national average on tests. Kentucky also had a below-average number of high school graduates.

In 1990, the state government passed the Kentucky Education Reform Act to help improve education. This law provides money to train teachers and to purchase school equipment. Creating more preschool classes and building family service centers also is part of the plan.

Workers finished Kentucky's state capitol building in 1910.

# Chapter 4

# Government and Politics

Each state has a government run by the consent of its people. This type of government is called a commonwealth. Kentucky is one of only four states to officially call itself a commonwealth. Kentucky's official name is the Commonwealth of Kentucky.

## State Government

Under Kentucky's state constitution, its government is divided into three branches. These branches are the executive, the legislative, and the judicial.

The executive branch carries out laws. The governor is the head of this branch. Kentuckians elect their governor to a four-year term. They also elect several other officers, including

*"I know my duty and coming from a slave state as I do, no power on Earth shall ever make me vote for the extension of slavery over one foot of territory now free. Never. No, sir. NO!"*

*—Henry Clay, U.S. Congressman from Kentucky*

the lieutenant governor, the secretary of state, and the attorney general. The executive branch also includes 14 cabinets. These departments oversee the governor's state policies.

The legislative branch makes state laws. Kentucky's legislature is called the General Assembly. The General Assembly is divided into the senate and the house of representatives. Senators are elected to four-year terms. Representatives are elected to two-year terms.

Kentucky's judicial branch is made up of four different levels. Most of the state's legal matters, criminal cases, and civil cases are decided by district courts. Circuit courts hear cases involving serious crimes and large amounts of money. The court of appeals reviews decisions made by the lower courts. The supreme court in Kentucky has say over all lower court rulings.

## Local Government

Kentucky has 120 counties. Kentucky has more counties than all other states except Texas.

# Kentucky's State Government

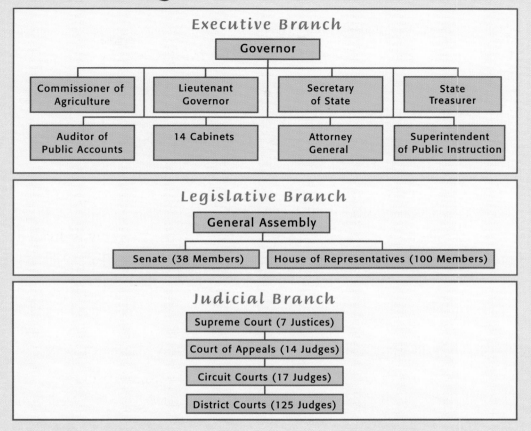

**Executive Branch**

Governor

| Commissioner of Agriculture | Lieutenant Governor | Secretary of State | State Treasurer |
| Auditor of Public Accounts | 14 Cabinets | Attorney General | Superintendent of Public Instruction |

**Legislative Branch**

General Assembly

Senate (38 Members) · House of Representatives (100 Members)

**Judicial Branch**

Supreme Court (7 Justices)

Court of Appeals (14 Judges)

Circuit Courts (17 Judges)

District Courts (125 Judges)

Counties' executive, legislative, and judicial powers are represented by fiscal courts. These government organizations often are run by a county judge executive and several law officers. Some counties elect a county judge executive and a board of commissioners to oversee local government. County governments help maintain roads and provide money for public schools.

## Federal Government

In the 1800s, Cassius Marcellus Clay from Kentucky co-founded the Republican Party. The party's main goal was to keep slavery out of the western territories. Today, the Republican Party is one of two major political parties in the United States.

Many Kentuckians have served in federal government. Richard Johnson, John Breckinridge, Adlai Stevenson, and Alben Barkley have served as vice presidents. Presidents Zachary Taylor and Abraham Lincoln both lived in Kentucky. Frederick Vinson, John Harlan, and Louis Brandeis have served on the U.S. Supreme Court.

Zachary Taylor was born in Virginia and raised in Kentucky. He was a general during the Mexican War (1846–1848) before serving as the 12th U.S. president.

# Henry Clay

Henry Clay was one of Kentucky's most important politicians. Born in Virginia, he moved to Lexington in 1797. In 1803, Clay was elected to the Kentucky state legislature.

In 1810, Clay was elected to the U.S. House of Representatives. There, he became a member of the War Hawks. This group of Congressmen wanted to go to war with Great Britain. They helped bring about the War of 1812 (1812–1814).

Later, Clay became known as the "Great Compromiser." He supported two laws that eased tension between slave and free, or nonslave, states. The Missouri Compromise of 1820 allowed Missouri to enter the union as a slave state and Maine to enter as a free state. The Compromise of 1850 made California a free state. It also allowed the territories of Utah and New Mexico to practice slavery.

Clay unsuccessfully ran for president several times. He served as Secretary of State for President John Quincy Adams. He also was elected to the U.S. Senate. Henry Clay died in 1852.

Tobacco is one of Kentucky's most important crops.

# Chapter 5

# Economy and Resources

Since the state's founding, Kentucky's economy has gone through many changes. Kentucky's main industry throughout the 1700s and 1800s was agriculture. People farmed hemp, corn, and tobacco. Kentucky did not develop its manufacturing industries until the mid-1900s, which is later than most other states. Today, service industries and mining are important parts of Kentucky's economy.

## Agriculture

Agriculture decreased in importance after World War II. By 1990, less than 4 percent of Kentuckians worked on farms.

But tobacco is still a major source of income for Kentucky. Kentucky grows nearly one-quarter of the U.S. tobacco crop. Other crops grown in the state include corn, soybeans, and wheat.

Livestock are important to Kentucky's agricultural industry. The Bluegrass Region is famous for thoroughbred horses. These fast horses are bred for racing. Other livestock raised in Kentucky include cattle, chickens, hogs, and sheep.

## Manufacturing

Manufacturing did not become Kentucky's main industry until the mid- to late 1900s. Kentucky's large coal deposits and hydroelectric plants provide low energy costs and helped draw companies to the state.

Cars and trucks are Kentucky's leading manufactured products. In 1988, Toyota opened its first plant in the United States in Georgetown. Chevrolet's Corvette sports cars are manufactured in Bowling Green. Ford builds trucks in Louisville.

Horses, such as thoroughbreds, are raised in Kentucky's Bluegrass Region.

More than one-fourth of Kentucky's manufacturing jobs are located in Louisville. Factories in Louisville produce cars, trucks, home appliances, and tobacco products.

Bourbon is another important manufacturing product. Kentucky is one of the world's largest producers of bourbon.

Factories in Louisville produce home appliances like washing machines.

This special type of whiskey is named after Bourbon County in Kentucky.

## Service Industries

Nearly 25 percent of Kentucky's jobs are in service industries. Doctors, lawyers, nurses, government workers, and teachers are service workers. Hotels and retail stores are other sources of service industry jobs.

Tourism is an important service industry. Kentucky has more than 50 state parks. Parks and other attractions draw many visitors. Tourists spend almost $4 billion in Kentucky each year.

Many Kentuckians work in federal and local government. The largest centers of government are in Frankfort, Lexington, and Louisville. Large army bases like Fort Campbell and Fort Knox employ many people. Some government workers operate dams for the Tennessee Valley Authority.

## Mining

Coal is Kentucky's most important mining product. Kentucky is one of the nation's leading coal-producing states. Coal deposits lie under 40 percent of Kentucky's land. Most coal is mined in the Western Coal Field and the Appalachian Plateau.

Oil, natural gas, limestone, and clay are other natural resources mined in Kentucky. Oil and natural gas deposits lie near many coal fields and in the southern part of the Mississippi Plateau. Limestone is found in northern Kentucky. Large deposits of clay lie underground in the Jackson Purchase area.

These workers are drilling for oil in Kentucky.

# Colonel Sanders

Colonel Harland Sanders was born September 9, 1890, in Indiana. When he was 40, Sanders bought a gas station in Corbin, Kentucky, and started cooking for travelers. One of his most popular dishes was fried chicken. As business improved, Sanders started a restaurant. His food became so popular that Governor Ruby Laffon made him an honorary Kentucky colonel in 1935.

In 1952, Sanders began to travel the country to start his Kentucky Fried Chicken (KFC) restaurant chain. He would cook chicken for restaurant owners. If they liked it, they would agree to pay Sanders a nickel for each piece of chicken they sold using his recipe.

By 1964, more than 600 restaurants sold Sanders' chicken. That same year, Sanders sold his company for $2 million.

Sanders remained the public spokesperson for KFC. Even after his death in 1980, the face of Colonel Harland Sanders still appears on every KFC box.

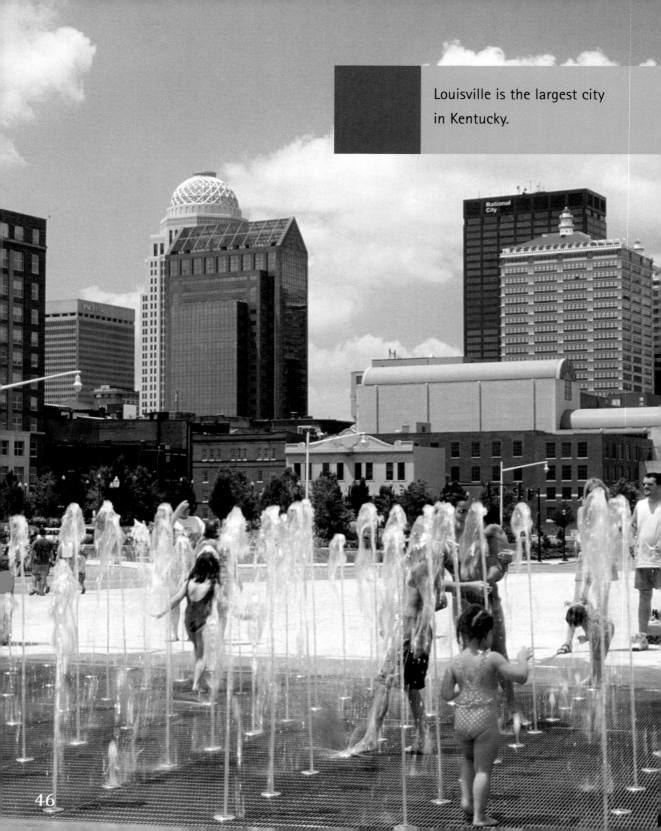

Louisville is the largest city in Kentucky.

# Chapter 6

# People and Culture

More than 4 million people live in Kentucky today. It is the 25th most populated state. Slightly more than half of Kentuckians live in cities. Kentucky's largest cities include Louisville, Lexington, Owensboro, and Bowling Green. Most of the state's rural population lives in the western and southern parts of the state. Few people live in the Appalachian Plateau.

## People

Most Kentuckians come from European backgrounds. About 90 percent of the people in Kentucky are white. Many of these people have English, Scottish, or German backgrounds.

Kentucky has several other ethnic groups. The state's African American population includes descendants of former slaves. Kentucky's Hispanic population has almost doubled from 1990 to 2000. Asian Americans have moved to Kentucky from China, India, and the Philippines. Kentucky's American Indian population descended from Cherokee, Shawnee, and Creek Indians.

## Arts

Kentucky has many museums. The J.B. Speed Art Museum in Louisville is known for its exhibits of European art, American

American sculptor Alexander Calder made *The Red Feather* in 1975. It stands outside the Kentucky Center for the Arts.

# Kentucky's Ethnic Background

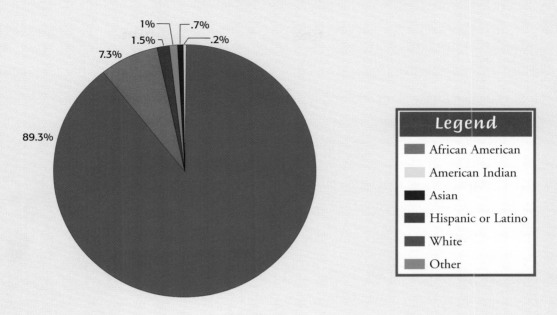

1%
.7%
1.5%
.2%
7.3%
89.3%

**Legend**
- African American
- American Indian
- Asian
- Hispanic or Latino
- White
- Other

Indian items, and Kentucky art. Other well-known museums include the University of Kentucky Art Museum, the Kentucky Historical Society museums, the Louisville Science Center, and the Kentucky Center for the Arts.

Several famous musicians come from Kentucky. Loretta Lynn is one of Kentucky's most famous musicians. Her father was a Kentucky coal miner. Naomi Judd, Wynonna Judd,

# Bluegrass Music

Bluegrass is a popular type of music in Kentucky. Bluegrass bands usually include a singer, a fiddler, a bass player, and a mandolin or guitar player. Musicians play songs about home, love, and family. These songs often are played with a fast beat.

Originally called "old-time country music," bluegrass began in the south as settlers moved across the Appalachian Mountains. Bluegrass is a mix of music styles that were popular with farm families. It also was influenced by blues, gospel music, and folk music of European immigrants.

William Smith "Bill" Monroe is considered the father of bluegrass. He was born in Kentucky in 1911. He learned to sing and to play mandolin. In the late 1930s, he formed the Blue Grass Boys. Playing at the Grand Ole Opry in Nashville, Tennessee, Monroe and his band became popular. Their style of music became known as "bluegrass." They had several hit songs including "Blue Moon of Kentucky" and "I'm Going Back to Old Kentucky."

Rosemary Clooney, the Everly Brothers, and Lionel Hampton are other famous Kentucky musicians.

## Sports

Horse racing is popular in Kentucky. Churchill Downs is one of the largest racehorse tracks in the country. Other Kentucky racetracks include Keeneland, Turfway Park, and Ellis Park.

Kentucky is known for its college basketball teams. The University of Kentucky Wildcats have won several national championships. Wildcat games against the University of Louisville Cardinals draw large crowds from around the state.

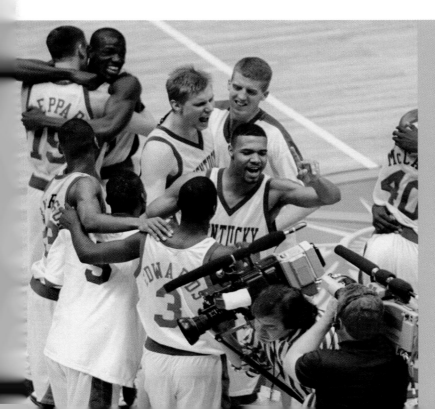

The Kentucky Wildcats beat the Syracuse Orangemen to win the 1996 NCAA Basketball Championship.

## Sites to See

Kentucky is home to many parks and natural wonders. The Land Between the Lakes National Recreation Area is one of the largest parks in the state. Visitors to Cumberland Falls in eastern Kentucky can see one of the only waterfalls in North America that makes a moonbow. A moonbow has colors similar to a rainbow. But the moon, not the sun, is the light source for the moonbow's colors. Many visitors to Kentucky also enjoy steamboat rides on the Ohio River.

Kentucky is home to many famous historical sites. Visitors to Hodgenville can see the cabin where Abraham Lincoln was

born. Visitors to the Cumberland Gap National Historic Park can walk along the same trail that Daniel Boone used to lead settlers into Kentucky. The Blue Licks Battlefield Resort stands on the area where Kentucky's bloodiest battle of the Revolutionary War was fought.

The richness of Kentucky's land and history make it an interesting state to visit. Horse racing fans flock to Kentucky's racetracks in spring and summer. Thousands more come year-round to tour the state's historic sites and view its scenery.

Visitors to Kentucky can take steamboat rides on the Ohio River.

# Recipe: Kentucky Derby Pie

*People make several versions of chocolate pecan pie, such as "famous horse race pie," "Bluegrass pie," "thoroughbred pie," or "Kentucky Derby pie." These pies are eaten around the time of the Kentucky Derby. People also make them for holidays like Christmas and Easter.*

## Ingredients

2 9-inch (23-centimeter) unbaked pie crusts
1½ cups (360 mL) sugar
¾ cup (175 mL) flour
3 eggs
¾ cup (175 mL) melted butter
1½ cups (360 mL) chopped pecans
1½ cups (360 mL) semi-sweet chocolate chips
1½ teaspoons (7.5 mL) vanilla extract

## Equipment

2 9-inch (23-centimeter) pie pans
nonstick cooking spray
2 medium mixing bowls
dry-ingredient measuring cups
mixing spoons
wire whisk
measuring spoons
pot holders
wire cooling rack

## What You Do

1. Preheat oven to 325°F (160°C).

2. Spray inside of pie pans with nonstick cooking spray. Place pie crusts in pie pans. Set aside.

3. Mix sugar and flour in medium mixing bowl.

4. With wire whisk, beat eggs and melted butter in second mixing bowl. Then stir egg mixture into sugar and flour mixture.

5. Stir in pecans, chocolate chips, and vanilla extract into pie mixture.

6. Pour equal amounts of pie mix into the two pie crusts and spread out evenly with a mixing spoon.

7. Bake 40 to 45 minutes.

8. Remove from oven and let cool on wire cooling rack.

Makes 2 pies

# Kentucky's Flag and Seal

## Kentucky's Flag

Kentucky's state flag features the state seal in the middle of a navy blue background.

## Kentucky's State Seal

A pioneer shakes hands with a statesman in the middle of Kentucky's state seal. The pioneer represents Kentucky's frontier settlers. The statesman represents Kentuckians who served in state and federal government. The state motto, "United we stand, divided we fall," circles the two figures. The motto comes from "Liberty Song," by John Dickinson. Across the top of the seal is written "Commonwealth of Kentucky," the official state name. The flowers across the bottom of the seal are goldenrod, the state flower.

# Almanac

**Nickname:** The Bluegrass State

**Population:** 4,041,789 (U.S. Census 2000)
**Population rank:** 25th

**Capital city:** Frankfort

**Largest cities:** Louisville, Lexington, Owensboro, Bowling Green, Covington

**Agricultural products:** Tobacco, corn, soybeans, wheat

**Livestock:** Thoroughbreds, cattle, chickens, hogs, sheep

**Average summer temperature:** 75 degrees Fahrenheit (24 degrees Celsius)

**Average winter temperature:** 36 degrees Fahrenheit (2 degrees Celsius)

**Average annual precipitation:** 47 inches (119 centimeters)

**Area:** 40,411 square miles (104,664 square kilometers)
**Size rank:** 37th

**Highest point:** Black Mountain, 4,139 feet (1,262 meters) above sea level

**Lowest point:** Along the Mississippi River, 257 feet (78 meters) above sea level

Thoroughbred

Goldenrod

Bird: Kentucky cardinal

Butterfly: Viceroy

Fish: Kentucky bass

Flower: Goldenrod

Fossil: Brachiopod

**Economy**

Natural resources: Coal, oil, natural gas, clay, limestone

Types of industry: Cars, trucks, home appliances, tobacco products, bourbon, tourism

**Symbols**

Gemstone: Freshwater pearl

Horse: Thoroughbred

Song: "My Old Kentucky Home," by Stephen C. Foster

Tree: Tulip tree

Wild animal: Gray squirrel

First governor: Isaac Shelby

Statehood: June 1, 1792, (15th state)

U.S. Representatives: 6

U.S. Senators: 2

U.S. electoral votes: 8

Counties: 120

**Government**

# Timeline

## State History

**1654**
Abraham Wood makes the first recorded trip to Kentucky. At the time, Cherokee, Chickasaw, Shawnee, Creek, and Mingo Indians live and hunt in the area.

**1750**
Thomas Walker enters Kentucky through the Cumberland Gap.

**1792**
Kentucky becomes the 15th state.

**1818**
Kentucky expands its borders due to the Jackson Purchase.

**1875**
The first Kentucky Derby is run at Churchill Downs.

## U.S. History

**1620**
Pilgrims establish a colony in North America.

**1775–1783**
American colonists fight for their freedom in the Revolutionary War.

**1812–1814**
The United States and Great Britain fight the War of 1812.

**1861–1865**
The Civil War is fought between Northern and Southern states.

**1904**

The Black Patch War between tobacco farmers and tobacco companies occurs.

**2000**

Coal waste spill pollutes eastern Kentucky rivers and streams.

**1990**

Kentucky's legislature passes the Kentucky Education Reform Act.

**1933**

The Tennessee Valley Authority begins building dams in Kentucky.

**1988**

Toyota opens its first U.S. plant in Georgetown, Kentucky.

**1929–1939**

The United States' economy suffers the Great Depression.

**1964**

U.S. Congress passes the Civil Rights Act, which makes discrimination illegal.

**1914–1918**

World War I is fought; the United States enters the war in 1917.

**1939–1945**

World War II is fought; the United States enters the war in 1941.

**2001**

On September 11, terrorists attack the World Trade Center and the Pentagon.

# Words to Know

commonwealth (KOM-uhn-welth)—a type of government in which the people have a right to make laws

compromise (KOM-pruh-mize)—to reach an agreement between two different ideas

descendant (di-SEND-uhnt)—a person's children and family members born after those children

erosion (e-ROH-zhuhn)—the wearing away of land by water or wind

executive (eg-ZEK-yuh-tiv)—having to do with the branch of government that enacts laws

hydroelectricity (hye-droh-ee-lek-TRISS-uh-tee)—electricity made from energy produced by running water

integration (in-tuh-GRAY-shuhn)—the practice of including people of all races

legislature (LEJ-iss-lay-chur)—a group of people who have the power to make or change laws

segregation (seg-ruh-GAY-shuhn)—the practice of keeping people or things apart from another group

thoroughbred (THUR-oh-bred)—any racehorse of a breed derived from a crossing of domestic English stock with Arabian stock

# To Learn More

**Boraas, Tracey.** *Daniel Boone: Frontier Scout.* Let Freedom Ring. Mankato, Minn: Bridgestone Books, 2003.

**Brown, Dottie**. *Kentucky.* Hello U.S.A. Minneapolis: Lerner, 2002.

**Kummer, Patricia K.** *Kentucky.* One Nation. Mankato, Minn.: Capstone Press, 2003.

**Stein, R. Conrad**. *Kentucky.* America the Beautiful. New York: Children's Press, 1999.

# Internet Sites

Track down many sites about Kentucky.
Visit the FACT HOUND at *http://www.facthound.com*

IT IS EASY!  IT IS FUN!

1) Go to http://*www.facthound.com*
2) Type in: 0736815856
3) Click on "FETCH IT"
   and FACT HOUND will find
   several links hand-picked by our editors.

Relax and let our pal FACT HOUND do the research for you!

# Places to Write and Visit

**Bluegrass Heritage Museum**
217 South Main Street
Winchester, KY  40391

**Kentucky Department of Parks**
Capital Plaza Tower
500 Mero Street
Suite 1100
Frankfort, KY  40601-1974

**Mammoth Cave National Park**
P.O. Box 7
Mammoth Cave, KY  42259

**National Corvette Museum**
350 Corvette Drive
Bowling Green, KY  42101

The Shakers were a religious group that came to Kentucky in the early 1800s. This photo shows a woman reenacting the Shaker's simple way of living.

# Index